# Air Fryer Cookbook Meat Recipes

*Air Fryer Meat Recipes with Low Salt, Low Fat and Less Oil.*
*The Healthier Way to Enjoy Deep-Fried Flavours*

**Ronda Williams**

# Table of Contents

# 1. <u>Air Fryer Chicken Fried Steak</u>

Prep Time: 20 minutes

Cook Time: 8 minutes

Total Time: 28 minutes

**Ingredients**

**For The Steaks**

- 2 cube steaks, 5-6 ounces each
- 3/4 cup All-Purpose Flour
- 1 teaspoon Ground Black Pepper
- 1 teaspoon Kosher Salt
- 1/2 teaspoon smoked paprika
- 1/2 teaspoon Onion Powder
- 1/2 teaspoon garlic powder
- 1/4 teaspoon Cayenne Pepper
- 2 teaspoons crumbled dried sage

- 3/4 cup buttermilk
- 1 teaspoon hot pepper sauce
- 1 Egg
- Non-Stick Cooking Spray

**For The Gravy**

- 4 tablespoons butter
- 2 tablespoons All-Purpose Flour
- 1 teaspoon Cracked Black Pepper
- 1/2 teaspoon Kosher Salt
- 1/4 teaspoon garlic salt
- 1/2 cup Whole Milk
- 1/2 cup Heavy Cream

## Instructions

### Steaks

- For the flour dredge, mix together in a shallow bowl, whisk the flour, 1 teaspoon pepper, 1 teaspoon salt, paprika, onion powder, garlic powder, cayenne, and sage.
- In a separate shallow bowl, whisk the buttermilk, hot pepper sauce, and egg.
- Pat the steaks dry with a paper towel. Season to taste with salt and pepper. Allow standing for 5 minutes, then pat dry again with a paper towel.
- Dredge the steaks in the seasoned flour mixture, shaking off any excess. Then dredge in the buttermilk mixture, allowing excess to drip off. Dredge in the flour mixture again, shaking off excess. Place the breaded steaks on a sheet pan and press any remaining flour mixture onto the steaks, making sure that each steak is completely coated. Let stand for 10 minutes.
- Place steaks in the air fryer basket. Lightly coat with vegetable oil spray. Set the air fryer to 400°F for 8 minutes, carefully turning steaks and coating the other side with vegetable oil spray halfway through the cooking time.

### Gravy

- Meanwhile, for the gravy: In a small saucepan, melt the butter over low heat. Whisk in the flour, pepper, salt, and garlic salt, continually whisking.
- Slowly add the milk and cream mixture, whisking constantly. Turn the heat to medium and cook, whisking occasionally, until thickened.
- Use a meat thermometer to ensure the steaks have reached an internal temperature of 145°F. Serve the steaks topped with the gravy.

**Nutrition Facts**

- Calories: 787kcal | Carbohydrates: 54g | Protein: 51g | Fat: 40g | Fiber: 2g | Sugar: 11g

# 2. Air Fryer Korean BBQ Beef

Prep Time: 15 Minutes

Cook Time: 30 Minutes

Total Time: 45 Minutes

**Ingredients**

Meat

- 1 Pound Flank Steak or Thinly Sliced Steak
- 1/4 Cup Corn Starch
- Pompeian Oils Coconut Spray

**Sauce**

- 1/2 Cup Soy Sauce or Gluten-Free Soy Sauce

- 1/2 Cup Brown Sugar
- 2 Tbsp Pompeian White Wine Vinegar
- 1 Clove Garlic, Crushed
- 1 Tbsp Hot Chili Sauce
- 1 Tsp Ground Ginger
- 1/2 Tsp Sesame Seeds
- 1 Tbsp Cornstarch
- 1 Tbsp Water

## Instructions

- Begin by preparing the steak. Thinly slice it then toss in the cornstarch.
- Spray the basket or line it with foil in the air fryer with coconut oil spray.
- Add the steak and spray another coat of spray on top.
- Cook in the air fryer for 10 minutes at 390*, turn the steak, and cook for an additional 10 minutes.
- While the steak is cooking add the sauce ingredients EXCEPT for the cornstarch and water to a medium saucepan.
- Warm it up to a low boil, then whisk in the cornstarch and water.
- Carefully remove the steak and pour the sauce over the steak, mix well.
- Serve topped with sliced green onions, cooked rice, and green beans.

## Nutrition Information

- Total Fat: 22g| Saturated Fat: 10g| Trans Fat: 0g| Unsaturated Fat: 10g|Cholesterol: 113mg| Sodium: 1531mg| Carbohydrates: 32g| Fiber: 2g| Sugar: 21g| Protein: 39g

# 3. **Air Fryer Mongolian Beef**

Prep Time: 20 Minutes

Cook Time: 20 Minutes

Total Time: 40 Minutes

**Ingredients**

**Meat**

- 1 Lb Flank Steak
- 1/4 Cup Corn Starch

**Sauce**

- 2 Tsp Vegetable Oil
- 1/2 Tsp Ginger
- 1 Tbsp Minced Garlic
- 1/2 Cup Soy Sauce or Gluten Free Soy Sauce

- 1/2 Cup Water
- 3/4 Cup Brown Sugar Packed

**Extras**

- Cooked Rice
- Green Beans
- Green Onions

**Instructions**

- Thinly slice the steak into long pieces, then coat with the corn starch.
- Place in the Air Fryer and cook on 390* for 5 minutes on each side. (Start with 5 minutes and add more time if needed. I cook this for 10 minutes on each side; however, others have suggested that was too long for theirs.)
- While the steak cooks, warm up all sauce ingredients in a medium sized saucepan on medium-high heat.
- Whisk the ingredients together until it gets to a low boil.
- Once both the steak and sauce are cooked, place the steak in a bowl with the sauce and let it soak in for about 5-10 minutes.
- When ready to serve, use tongs to remove the steak and let the excess sauce drip off.
- Place steak on cooked rice and green beans, top with additional sauce if you prefer.

**Nutrition Information:**

- Total Fat: 16g| Saturated Fat: 5g| Trans Fat: 0g| Unsaturated Fat: 8g| Cholesterol: 116mg| Sodium: 2211mg| Carbohydrates: 57g| Fiber: 1g| Sugar: 35g| Protein: 44g

# 4. <u>Air Fryer Beef And Bean Taquitos</u>

Prep Time: 10 Minutes

Cook Time: 15 Minutes

Total Time: 25 Minutes

## Ingredients

- 1 Pound Ground Beef
- 1 Package Gluten-Free or Regular Taco Seasoning
- 1 Can of Refried Beans
- 1 Cup Shredded Sharp Cheddar
- 20 White Corn Tortillas

## Instructions

- Begin by preparing the ground beef if it isn't already.
- Brown the meat on medium-high heat and add in the taco seasoning per the instructions on the package.
- Once you are done with the meat, heat up the corn tortillas for about 30 seconds.
- Spray the air fryer basket with non-stick cooking spray or add a sheet of foil and spray.
- Add ground beef, beans, and a bit of cheese to each tortilla.
- Wrap them tightly and place seam side down in the air fryer.
- Add a quick spray of cooking oil spray, such as olive oil cooking spray.
- Cook at 390 degrees for 12 minutes.
- Repeat for any additional tortillas.

## Nutrition Information:

- Total Fat: 9g| Saturated Fat: 4g| Trans Fat: 0g| Unsaturated Fat: 4g| Cholesterol: 31mg| Sodium: 207mg| Carbohydrates: 14g| Fiber: 2g| Sugar: 0g| Protein: 11g

# 5. <u>Air Fryer Steak Fajitas With Onions And Peppers</u>

Prep Time: 10 Minutes

Cook Time: 15 Minutes

Total Time: 25 Minutes

**Ingredients**

- 1 lb Thin Cut Steak

- 1 Green Bell Pepper Sliced
- 1 Yellow Bell Pepper Sliced
- 1 Red Bell Pepper Sliced
- 1/2 Cup White Onions Sliced
- 1 Packet Gluten Free Fajita Seasoning
- Olive Oil Spray
- Gluten-Free Corn Tortillas or Flour Tortillas

## Instructions

- Line the basket of the air fryer with foil and coat with spray.
- Thinly slice the steak against the grain, this should be about 1/4 inch slices.
- Mix the steak with peppers and onions.
- Add to the air fryer.
- Evenly coat with the fajita seasoning.
- Cook for 5 minutes on 390*.
- Mix up the steak mixture.
- Continue cooking for an additional 5-10 minutes until your desired doneness.
- Serve in warm tortillas.

## Nutrition Information:

- Total Fat: 17g | Saturated Fat: 6g | Trans Fat: 0g | Unsaturated Fat: 9g | Cholesterol: 73mg | Sodium: 418mg | Carbohydrates: 15g | Fiber: 2g | Sugar: 4g | Protein: 22g

# 6. <u>Air Fryer Meatballs (Low Carb)</u>

Prep Time: 10 minutes  Cook Time: 14 minutes  Total Time: 24 minutes

Servings: 3 -4

## Ingredients

- 1 lb Lean Ground Beef
- 1/4 Cup Marinara Sauce
- 1 Tablespoon Dried Minced Onion or Freeze Dried Shallots
- 1 teaspoon Minced Garlic I used freeze-dried
- 1 teaspoon Pizza Seasoning or Italian Seasoning
- 1/3 Cup Shredded Parmesan
- 1 Egg
- Salt and Pepper to taste
- Shredded Mozzarella Cheese optional
- 1 1/4 cups Marinara Sauce optional

## Instructions

- Mix together all ingredients except reserve 1 1/4 cup of the marinara sauce and the mozzarella cheese.
- Form mixture into 12 meatballs and place in a single layer in the air fryer basket.
- Cook in the air fryer at 350 for 11 minutes.
- Optional: Place meatballs in an air fryer pan, toss in remaining marinara sauce, and top with mozzarella cheese. Place air fryer pan into the basket and cook at 350 for 3 minutes.

## Nutritional Value

- Calories: 572kcal | Carbohydrates: 1g | Protein: 46g | Fat: 43g | Saturated Fat: 22g | Cholesterol: 168mg | Sodium: 219mg | Potassium: 606mg | Sugar: 1g | Vitamin A: 355IU | Calcium: 16mg | Iron: 4mg

# 7. **Air Fryer Roast Beef**

Prep Time: 5 mins

Cook Time: 35 mins

Total Time: 40 mins

**Ingredients**

- 2 lb beef roast top round or eye of round is best
- Oil for spraying
- Rub
- 1 tbs kosher salt
- 1 tsp black pepper
- 2 tsp garlic powder

- 1 tsp summer savory or thyme

**Instructions**

- Mix all rub ingredients and rub into the roast.
- Place fat side down in the basket of the air fryer (or set up for rotisserie if your air fryer is so equipped)
- Lightly spray with oil.
- Set fryer to 400 degrees F and air fry for 20 minutes; turn fat-side up and spray lightly with oil. Continue cooking for 15 additional minutes at 400 degrees F.
- Remove the roast from the fryer, tent with foil, and let the meat rest for 10 minutes.
- The time given should produce a rare roast which should be 125 degrees F on a meat thermometer. Additional time will be needed for medium, medium-well, and well. Always use a meat thermometer to test the temperature.
- Approximate times for medium and well respectively are 40 minutes and 45 minutes. Remember to always use a meat thermometer as times are approximate and fryers differ by wattage.

**Nutrition**

- Calories: 238kcal | Carbohydrates: 1g | Protein: 25g | Fat: 14g | Saturated Fat: 6g | Cholesterol: 89mg | Sodium: 1102mg | Potassium: 448mg | Vitamin A: 55IU | Vitamin C: 0.3mg | Calcium: 37mg | Iron: 3mg

# 8. <u>Air Fryer Stuffed Peppers</u>

Prep Time: 15 Minutes

Cook Time: 15 Minutes

Total Time: 30 Minutes

**Ingredients**

- 6 Green Bell Peppers
- 1 Lb Lean Ground Beef
- 1 Tbsp Olive Oil
- 1/4 Cup Green Onion Diced
- 1/4 Cup Fresh Parsley

- 1/2 Tsp Ground Sage
- 1/2 Tsp Garlic Salt
- 1 Cup Cooked Rice
- 1 Cup Marinara Sauce More to Taste
- 1/4 Cup Shredded Mozzarella Cheese

## Instructions

- Warm-up a medium-sized skillet with the ground beef and cook until well done.
- Drain the beef and return to the pan.
- Add in the olive oil, green onion, parsley, sage, and salt. Mix this well.
- Add in the cooked rice and marinara, mix well.
- Cut the top off of each pepper and clean the seeds out.
- Scoop the mixture into each of the peppers and place it in the basket of the air fryer. (I did 4 the first round, 2 the second to make them fit.)
- Cook for 10 minutes at 355*, carefully open and add cheese.
- Cook for an additional 5 minutes or until peppers are slightly soft and cheese is melted.
- Serve.

## Nutrition Information

- Total Fat: 13g | Saturated Fat: 4g | Trans Fat: 0g | Unsaturated Fat: 7g | Cholesterol: 70mg | Sodium: 419mg | Carbohydrates: 19g | Fiber: 2g | Sugar: 6g | Protein: 25g

# 9. Air Fryer Steak

Prep Time: 10 mins

Cook Time: 15 mins

Resting Time: 8 mins

Total Time: 30 mins

**Ingredients**

- 2 (10 to 12 ounces EACH) sirloin steaks, about one inch thick, and at room temperature which is important for proper and even cooking.
- ½ tablespoon olive oil OR olive oil cooking spray, for the steaks
- 1 tablespoon kosher salt
- 1 tablespoon garlic powder
- 1 tablespoon onion powder
- ½ tablespoon paprika, sweet or smoked
- ½ tablespoon freshly ground black pepper
- 2 teaspoons dried herbs of choice

**Instructions**

- Preheat Air Fryer to 400°F.
- Rub both steaks with olive oil, or spray with cooking spray, and set aside.
- In a small mixing bowl combine salt, garlic powder, onion powder, paprika, pepper, and dried herbs. This makes enough seasoning for about 4 large steaks.
- Rub preferred amount of seasoning all over the steaks. Store leftover seasoning blends in a small airtight container and keeps it in a cool, dry place.
- Place 1 steak in the Air Fryer basket and cook for 6 minutes at 400°F.
- If you have a bigger Air Fryer, both steaks can fit in at the same time, but just make sure they aren't one on top of the other. You want a little space between the two.
- Flip over the steak and continue to cook for 4 to 5 more minutes, or until cooked through.

- Please use an Instant Read Thermometer to check for doneness; for a RARE steak, the temperature should register at 125°F to 130°F. For Medium-Rare, you want an internal temperature of 135°F.
- IF the steak isn't cooked through, it may be too thick and you'll want to return the steak to the air fryer and give it a minute or two to finish cooking.
- Repeat the cooking method with the other steak.
- Remove from air fryer and let rest for 5 to 8 minutes before cutting.
- Serve with a pat of butter and garnish with chopped parsley.

**Nutrition Facts**

- Fat: 17g
- Saturated Fat: 5g
- Cholesterol: 173mg
- Sodium: 3656mg
- Potassium: 1112mg
- Carbohydrates: 8g
- Fiber: 2g
- Sugar: 1g
- Protein: 64g
- Calcium: 99mg
- Iron: 5mg

# 10.   **Air Fryer Steak Fajitas**

Prep Time: 10 mins

Cook Time: 10 mins

Total Time: 20 mins

**Ingredients**

- 2 pounds flank steak strips
- 1 packet taco seasoning
- 1/2 red bell pepper, seeded, cored, and sliced
- 1/2 yellow bell pepper, seeded, cored, and sliced
- 1 onion, peeled and sliced
- 2 tablespoons freshly squeezed lime juice
- Cooking spray
- Flour tortillas
- Cilantro, chopped

## Instructions

- Season steak with taco seasoning. Marinate for about 20 to 30 minutes.
- Preheat your air fryer to 400 degrees. Spray the air fryer tray with cooking spray,
- Arrange the seasoned beef on the air fryer tray, cooking in batches depending on the size of the air fryer.
- Add a layer of the sliced onions and a layer of bell peppers on top of the meat.
- Place in the air fryer for 10 minutes. Toss halfway through cooking to ensure the steak is cooked evenly.
- Remove from the air fryer and drizzle with lime juice.
- Serve in warm tortillas with fresh cilantro.

## Nutrition

- Calories: 620kcal | Carbohydrates: 56g | Protein: 56g | Fat: 17g | Saturated Fat: 6g | Cholesterol: 136mg | Sodium: 1446mg | Potassium: 1014mg | Fiber: 5g | Sugar: 8g | Vitamin A: 1350IU | Vitamin C: 55mg | Calcium: 149mg | Iron: 7mg

# 11.  Air Fryer Taco Calzones

Prep Time: 10 Minutes  Cook Time: 10 Minutes

Total Time: 20 Minutes

## Ingredients

- 1 tube Pillsbury thin crust pizza dough
- 1 cup taco meat
- 1 cup shredded cheddar

## Instructions

- Spread out your sheet of pizza dough on a clean surface. Using a pizza cutter, cut the dough into 4 even squares.
- Cut each square into a large circle using the pizza cutter. Set the dough scraps aside to make cinnamon sugar bites.
- Top one half of each circle of dough with 1/4 cup taco meat and 1/4 cup shredded cheese.
- Fold the empty half over the meat and cheese and press the edges of the dough together with a fork to seal it tightly. Repeat with all four calzones.
- Gently pick up each calzone and spray it with pan spray or olive oil. Arrange them in your Air Fryer basket.
- Cook the calzones at 325° for 8-10 minutes. Watch them closely at the 8-minute mark so you don't overcook them.
- Serve with salsa and sour cream.
- To make cinnamon sugar bites, cut the scraps of dough into even-sized pieces, about 2 inches long. Add them to the Air Fryer basket and cook at 325° for 5 minutes. Immediately toss with a 1:4 cinnamon-sugar mixture.

## Nutrition Information

- Total Fat: 31g| Saturated Fat: 14g| Trans Fat: 1g| Unsaturated Fat: 14g| Cholesterol: 58mg| Sodium: 814mg| Carbohydrates: 38g| Fiber: 2g| Sugar: 1g| Protein: 18g

# 12.  Jalapeno Lime Air Fryer Steak

Prep Time: 5 mins

Cook Time: 10 mins

Marinate Time: 30 mins

Total Time: 45 mins

Servings: 4

**Ingredients**

- 1 lb flank steak used flat iron – check keywords
- 1 lime juice and zest
- 1 jalapeno, sliced
- 3 cloves of garlic, minced
- 1/2 cup fresh cilantro, roughly chopped

- 2 tablespoons light brown sugar
- 1/2 teaspoon paprika
- 1/2 teaspoon fresh cracked pepper
- 1/4 cup avocado oil
- Salt

## Instructions

- Preheat the air fryer to 400F.
- Season the steak with salt and pepper. In a large mixing bowl, combine the avocado oil, paprika, pepper, brown sugar, cilantro, garlic, jalapeño, and lime zest from 1 lime. Add the steak and toss to coat. Marinate for 30 minutes.
- Air fry for 10 minutes for medium-rare, flipping the steak halfway through. When the steak is finished cooking, squeeze lime juice from half a lime over it. Allow it to rest with the air fryer lid open for 10 minutes before slicing. Serve the steak with steamed veggies, over a salad, or in a taco.

## Oven Instructions

- To make the steak in the oven, preheat the broiler on high and cook for 6 minutes for medium-rare. Squeeze lime juice from half a lime over the steak and allow it to rest for 10 minutes before slicing. Serve the steak with steamed veggies, over a salad, or in a taco.

## Nutrition

- Calories: 312kcal | Carbohydrates: 10g | Protein: 25g | Fat: 19g | Saturated Fat: 4g | Cholesterol: 68mg | Sodium: 64mg | Potassium: 432mg | Fiber: 1g | Sugar: 6g | Vitamin A: 296IU | Vitamin C: 13mg | Calcium: 41mg | Iron: 2mg

# 13.   Air Fryer Ribeye Steak (Frozen + Fresh)

Prep Time: 5 Minutes

Cook Time: 10 Minutes

Additional Time: 30 Minutes

Total Time: 45 Minutes

**Ingredients**

- 8-ounce ribeye steak, about 1-inch thick
- 1 tablespoon McCormick Montreal Steak Seasoning

**Instructions**

- Remove the ribeye steak from the fridge and season with the Montreal Steak seasoning. Let steak rest for about 20 minutes to come to room temperature (to get a more tender juicy steak).
- Preheat your air fryer to 400 degrees.
- Place the ribeye steak in the air fryer and cook for 10-12 minutes, until it reaches 130-135 degrees for medium-rare. Cook for an additional 5 minutes for medium-well.
- Remove the steak from the air fryer and let rest at least 5 minutes before cutting to keep the juices inside the steak then enjoy!

**Nutrition Information**

- Total Fat: 22g| Saturated Fat: 10g| Trans Fat: 0g| Unsaturated Fat: 12g| Cholesterol: 88mg| Sodium: 789mg| Carbohydrates: 2g| Fiber: 1g| Sugar: 0g| Protein: 29g

# 14. **Air Fryer Beef Chips**

Prep Time: 1 minute

Cook Time: 1 hour

Cooling Time: 5 minutes

Total Time: 1 hour 6 minutes

Servings: 2

**Ingredients**

- 1/2 lb Thinly Sliced Beef we recommend leaner cuts like sirloin
- 1/4 tsp Salt
- 1/4 tsp Black Pepper
- 1/4 tsp Garlic Powder

## Instructions

- Gather all the ingredients.
- In a small mixing bowl, combine salt, black pepper, garlic powder and mix well to create the seasoning.
- Lay the beef slices flat and sprinkle seasoning on both sides.
- Transfer beef into the air fryer tray single stacked (very important each slice is single stacked, otherwise they will not get crispy) and air fry for 45-60 minutes at 200F. Once done, let beef slices cool for 5 minutes before enjoying. Note - the time is going to vary greatly depending on thickness.

## Nutrition

- Calories: 290kcal | Carbohydrates: 1g | Protein: 20g | Fat: 23g | Saturated Fat: 9g | Cholesterol: 81mg | Sodium: 367mg | Potassium: 306mg | Sugar: 1g | Calcium: 20mg | Iron: 2mg

# 15. **Best Air Fryer Meatloaf With Tangy Sauce | Makes Two**

Prep Time: 9 Mins

Cook Time: 20 Mins

Resting Time: 5 Mins

Total Time: 34 Mins

## Ingredients

- 1 large egg
- 2 pounds ground chuck or a combination of ground beef and venison or ground sirloin
- 1/2 cup quick-cooking oats
- 3/4 teaspoon salt or garlic salt
- 1/4 teaspoon ground black pepper
- Tangy sauce
- 3/4 cup ketchup
- 2 tablespoons light brown sugar
- 1 tablespoon apple cider vinegar or white vinegar or rice vinegar
- 1 teaspoon worcestershire sauce or soy sauce or liquid amino liquid aminos are gluten-free

## Instructions

- To save washing another bowl, start by beating the egg in a large bowl with a fork.
- Break up the ground meat in the bowl. There's no getting around using your hands here. I usually use a pair of nylon/rubber gloves simply for easy cleanup. Gloves may be a luxury this day, though.
- Add quick-cooking oats, salt, and pepper.
- With your hands, gently mix in the egg, oats, salt, and pepper with the ground meat. Overworking the meat will make it tough. Under mixing may leave patches of oats or eggs not evenly incorporated.
- Shape the mixture into 2 free-form loaves, roughly 3 x 5.5 inches. The

30

size will depend on what will fit into your air fryer. (For conventional oven method, see the size in recipe notes) Carefully place the loaves side by side in the preheated air fryer basket or tray.

- Air fry or Roast for about 19 minutes or until meatloaves are done in the middle-firm when pressed in the middle of temperature on an instant-read thermometer reads 155°.
- It's a good idea to check at 17 minutes to make sure they aren't getting too brown. All air fryers are not alike.
- Prepare Tangy Sauce and Spread on Meatloaf
- Stir or whisk together ketchup, brown sugar, vinegar, and Worcestershire sauce.
- When meat waves are 155° or no pink shows in the center, evenly spread the Tangy Sauce over both meatloaves. Cook an additional 1 minute on Air Fry to set the sauce.
- Remove the meatloaves with silicone coated tongs if the air fryer basket is coated with a nonstick surface. Let the meatloaf stand on a cutting board or plate 5 minutes before slicing.

**Nutritional Value**

- Calories: 572kcal | Carbohydrates: 1g | Protein: 46g | Fat: 43g | Saturated Fat: 22g | Cholesterol: 168mg | Sodium: 219mg | Potassium: 606mg | Sugar: 1g | Vitamin A: 355IU | Calcium: 16mg | Iron: 4mg

# 16.   <u>Air Fryer Asian Beef & Veggies</u>

Prep Time: 10 minutes

Cook Time: 8 minutes

Total Time: 18 minutes

Servings: 4 people

**Ingredients**

- 1 lb sirloin steak cut into strips
- 2 tablespoons cornstarch (or arrowroot powder)
- 1/2 medium yellow onion, sliced
- 1 medium red pepper, sliced into strips
- 3 cloves garlic, minced
- 2 tablespoons grated ginger do not sub dry ground ginger
- 1/4 teaspoon red chili flakes
- 1/2 cup low sodium soy sauce
- 1/4 cup rice vinegar

- 1 tsp sesame oil
- 1/3 cup brown sugar
- 1 teaspoon chinese 5 spice optional
- 1/4 cup water

## Instructions

### For Freezer Prep

- Add all ingredients to a gallon-sized zip bag. Ensure all of the ingredients are combined.
- Label and freeze for up to 4 months.

### To Cook

- Thaw zip bag in the fridge overnight.
- Using tongs, remove the steak and veggies, and transfer to the Air Fryer. Discard the marinade.
- Set the Air Fryer to 400F and the timer to 8 minutes. I like to shake the basket halfway through, but I don't think it is necessary.
- Serve with rice, and garnish with sesame seeds and scallions.

### Nutrition

- Calories: 289kcal | Carbohydrates: 27g | Protein: 31g | Fat: 7g | Fiber: 1g | Sugar: 19g

# 17.   **Kofta Kebabs**

Prep Time: 45 mins Cook Time: 5 mins Additional Time: 30 mins Total Time: 1 hr 20 mins Servings: 28

**Ingredient**

- 4 cloves garlic, minced
- 1 teaspoon kosher salt
- 1 pound ground lamb
- 3 tablespoons grated onion
- 3 tablespoons chopped fresh parsley
- 1 tablespoon ground coriander
- 1 teaspoon ground cumin
- ½ tablespoon ground cinnamon
- ½ teaspoon ground allspice
- ¼ teaspoon cayenne pepper
- ¼ teaspoon ground ginger
- ¼ teaspoon ground black pepper
- 28 bamboo skewers, soaked in water for 30 minutes

**Instructions**

- Mash the garlic into a paste with the salt using a mortar and pestle or the flat side of a chef's knife on your cutting board. Mix the garlic into the lamb along with the onion, parsley, coriander, cumin, cinnamon, allspice, cayenne pepper, ginger, and pepper in a mixing bowl until well blended. Form the mixture into 28 balls. Form each ball around the tip of a skewer, flattening into a 2-inch oval; repeat with the remaining skewers. Place the kebabs onto a baking sheet, cover, and refrigerate for at least 30 minutes or up to 12 hours.
- Preheat an outdoor grill for medium heat, and lightly oil grate.
- Cook the skewers on the preheated grill, turning occasionally, until the lamb has cooked to your desired degree of doneness, about 6 minutes for medium.

**Nutrition Facts**

- Calories: 35; Protein 2.9g; Carbohydrates 0.6g; Fat 2.3g; Cholesterol

# 18.  <u>**Grilled Lamb Chops**</u>

Prep Time: 10 mins

Cook Time: 6 mins

Additional Time: 2 hrs

Total Time: 2 hrs 16 mins

Servings: 6

**Ingredient**

- ¼ cup distilled white vinegar
- 2 teaspoons salt
- ½ teaspoon black pepper
- 1 tablespoon minced garlic
- 1 onion, thinly sliced
- 2 tablespoons olive oil

- 2 pounds lamb chops

**Instructions**

- Mix together the vinegar, salt, pepper, garlic, onion, and olive oil in a large resealable bag until the salt has dissolved. Add lamb, toss until coated, and marinate in the refrigerator for 2 hours.
- Preheat an outdoor grill for medium-high heat.
- Remove lamb from the marinade and leave any onions on that stick to the meat. Discard any remaining marinade. Wrap the exposed ends of the bones with aluminum foil to keep them from burning. Grill to desired doneness, about 3 minutes per side for medium. The chops may also be broiled in the oven for about 5 minutes per side for medium.

**Nutrition Facts**

- Calories: 519; Protein 25g; Carbohydrates 2.3g; Fat 44.8g; Cholesterol 112mg; Sodium 861mg.

# 19.  Roast Leg Of Lamb

Prep Time: 15 mins

Cook Time: 1 hr 45 mins

Additional Time: 10 mins

Total Time: 2 hrs 10 mins

Servings: 12

## Ingredient

- 4 cloves garlic, sliced
- 2 tablespoons fresh rosemary
- Salt to taste
- Ground black pepper to taste
- 5 pounds leg of lamb

## Instructions

- Preheat oven to 350 degrees F (175 degrees C).
- Cut slits in the top of the leg of lamb every 3 to 4 inches, deep enough to push slices of garlic down into the meat. Salt and pepper generously all over the top of the lamb, place several sprigs of fresh rosemary under and on top of the lamb. Place lamb on roasting pan.
- Roast in the preheated oven until the lamb is cooked to your desired doneness, about 1 3/4 to 2 hours. Do not overcook the lamb, the flavor is best if the meat is still slightly pink. Let rest at least 10 minutes before carving.

## Nutrition Facts

- Calories: 382; Protein 35.8g; Carbohydrates 0.4g; Fat 25.3g; Cholesterol 136.1mg; Sodium 136.3mg.

# 20. <u>Roasted Lamb Breast</u>

Prep Time: 30 mins Cook Time: 2 hrs 25 mins Total Time: 2 hrs 55 mins
Servings: 4

**Ingredient**

- 2 tablespoons olive oil
- 2 teaspoons salt
- 2 teaspoons ground cumin
- 1 teaspoon freshly ground black pepper

- 1 teaspoon dried Italian herb seasoning
- 1 teaspoon ground cinnamon
- 1 teaspoon ground coriander
- 1 teaspoon paprika
- 4 pounds lamb breast, separated into two pieces
- ½ cup chopped Italian flat-leaf parsley
- ⅓ cup white wine vinegar, more as needed
- 1 lemon, juiced
- 2 cloves garlic, crushed
- 1 teaspoon honey
- ½ teaspoon red pepper flakes
- 1 pinch salt

## Instructions

- Preheat oven to 300 degrees F (150 degrees C).
- Combine chopped parsley, vinegar, fresh lemon juice, garlic, honey, red pepper flakes, and salt in a large bowl. Mix well and set aside.
- Whisk olive oil, salt, cumin, black pepper, dried Italian herbs, cinnamon, coriander, and paprika in a large bowl until combined.
- Coat each lamb breast in the olive oil and spice mixture and transfer to a roasting pan, fat side up.
- Tightly cover the roasting pan with aluminum foil and bake in the preheated oven until the meat is tender when pierced with a fork, about 2 hours.
- Remove lamb from the oven and cut into four pieces.
- Increase oven temperature to 450 degrees F (230 degrees C).
- Line a baking sheet with aluminum foil and place lamb pieces on it. Brush the tops of each piece with fat drippings from the roasting pan.
- Bake lamb until meat is browned and edges are crispy about 20 minutes.
- Increase the oven's broiler to high and brown lamb for 4 minutes. Remove from oven.
- Serve lamb topped with parsley and vinegar sauce.

## Nutrition Facts

- Calories: 622; Protein 46.2g; Carbohydrates 7.7g; Fat 45.3g; Cholesterol 180.4mg; Sodium 1301.6mg.

# 21.   <u>**Moroccan Lamb Stew With Apricots**</u>

Prep Time: 30 mins

Cook Time: 1 hr 55 mins

Total Time: 2 hrs 25 mins

Servings: 4

**Ingredient**

- 2 pounds boneless leg of lamb, cut into 1-inch cubes
- 2 teaspoons ground coriander
- 1 teaspoon ground cumin
- 1 teaspoon sweet paprika
- ½ teaspoon cayenne pepper
- ½ teaspoon ground cardamom

- ½ teaspoon ground turmeric
- 2 teaspoons kosher salt
- 2 tablespoons olive oil
- 2 cups finely chopped onion
- 4 cloves garlic, minced
- 1 tablespoon minced fresh ginger root
- 2 (3 inches) cinnamon sticks
- 2 cups low-sodium chicken stock
- 1 cup dried apricots, halved
- 2 (3 inches) orange peel strips
- 1 tablespoon honey
- ¼ cup chopped fresh cilantro
- ¼ cup toasted pine nuts

## Instructions

- Combine lamb, coriander, cumin, paprika, cayenne, cardamom, turmeric, and salt in a large bowl; toss together until lamb is evenly coated.
- Heat oil in a large Dutch oven or tagine over medium heat. Add onions; cook, stirring occasionally until soft and translucent, about 5 minutes. Stir in garlic, ginger, and cinnamon; cook, stirring frequently, until fragrant, about 1 minute. Add seasoned lamb; cook, stirring frequently until light brown, being careful not to caramelize, about 2 minutes. Add chicken stock and bring to a gentle boil over medium heat. Reduce heat to low and simmer, covered, until the lamb is just tender, about 1 hour and 15 minutes.
- Stir in apricots, orange peels, and honey; continue to simmer over low heat, uncovered, until the liquid has thickened slightly and lamb is fork-tender, about 30 minutes. Remove from the heat, discard cinnamon sticks and orange peels.
- Divide evenly among 4 bowls. Garnish each bowl with a tablespoon each of cilantro and pine nuts.

## Nutrition Facts

- Calories: 553; Protein 44.5g; Carbohydrates 40.9g; Fat 24.8g; Cholesterol 125.5mg; Sodium 1129.7mg.

# 22. Slow Cooker Lamb Chops

Prep Time: 15 mins

Cook Time: 4 hrs 30 mins

Additional Time: 5 mins

Total Time: 4 hrs 50 mins

Servings: 6

**Ingredient**

- ½ cup red wine
- ½ sweet onion, roughly chopped
- 3 tablespoons honey
- 2 tablespoons Dijon mustard
- 2 tablespoons lemon juice
- 4 garlic cloves, minced
- 1 tablespoon ground thyme
- 1 tablespoon dried rosemary
- 2 teaspoons ground basil
- 1 teaspoon salt
- 1 teaspoon coarse ground black pepper
- ¼ cup tapioca starch
- 1 ½ pound sirloin lamb chops, room temperature

**Instructions**

- Combine red wine and onion in a slow cooker.
- Whisk honey, mustard, lemon juice, garlic, thyme, rosemary, basil, salt, and pepper together in a small bowl until well blended. Add tapioca starch and whisk until well combined. Let sit until the mixture is thickened, at least 5 minutes.
- Dip lamb chops in the mustard mixture and massage until fully coated.
- Place chops in a single layer over the red wine and onion mixture in the slow cooker. Pour the remaining mustard mixture on top.

- Cover slow cooker and cook on Low until an instant-read thermometer inserted into the center of a chop reads at least 130 degrees F (54 degrees C), about 4 1/2 hours.

**Nutrition Facts**

- Calories: 209; Protein 13g; Carbohydrates 18.5g; Fat 7.7g; Cholesterol 43.6mg; Sodium 550.5mg.

# 23. Grilled Leg Of Lamb Steaks

Prep Time: 10 mins

Cook Time: 10 mins

Additional Time: 30 mins

Total: 50 mins

Servings: 4

**Ingredient**

- 4 bone-in lamb steaks
- ¼ cup olive oil
- 4 large cloves garlic, minced
- 1 tablespoon chopped fresh rosemary
- Salt and ground black pepper to taste

**Instructions**

- Place lamb steaks in a single layer in a shallow dish. Cover with olive oil, garlic, rosemary, salt, and pepper. Flip steaks to coat both sides. Let sit until steaks absorb flavors, about 30 minutes.
- Preheat an outdoor grill for high heat and lightly oil the grate. Cook steaks until browned on the outside and slightly pink in the center, about 5 minutes per side for medium. An instant-read thermometer inserted into the center should read at least 140 degrees F (60 degrees C).

**Nutrition Facts**

- Calories: 327; Protein 29.6g; Carbohydrates 1.7g; Fat 21.9g; Cholesterol 92.9mg; Sodium 112.1mg.

# 24.   Easy Meatloaf

Prep Time: 10 mins

Cook Time: 1 hr

Total Time: 1 hr 10 mins

Servings: 8

## Ingredient

- 1 ½ pounds ground beef
- 1 egg
- 1 onion, chopped
- 1 cup milk
- 1 cup dried bread crumbs
- Salt and pepper to taste
- 2 tablespoons brown sugar
- 2 tablespoons prepared mustard
- ⅓ cup ketchup

## Instructions

- Preheat oven to 350 degrees F (175 degrees C).
- In a large bowl, combine the beef, egg, onion, milk, and bread OR cracker crumbs. Season with salt and pepper to taste and place in a lightly greased 9x5-inch loaf pan, or form into a loaf and place in a lightly greased 9x13-inch baking dish.
- In a separate small bowl, combine the brown sugar, mustard, and ketchup. Mix well and pour over the meatloaf.
- Bake at 350 degrees F (175 degrees C) for 1 hour.

## Nutrition Facts

- Calories: 372; Protein 18.2g; Carbohydrates 18.5g; Fat 24.7g; Cholesterol 98mg; Sodium 334.6mg.

# 25. <u>Classic Meatloaf</u>

Prep: 30 mins

Cook: 45 mins

Total: 1 hr 15 mins

Servings: 10

**Meatloaf Ingredients:**

- 1 carrot, coarsely chopped

- 1 rib celery, coarsely chopped
- ½ onion, coarsely chopped
- ½ red bell pepper, coarsely chopped
- 4 white mushrooms, coarsely chopped
- 3 cloves garlic, coarsely chopped
- 2 ½ pounds ground chuck
- 1 tablespoon Worcestershire sauce
- 1 egg, beaten
- 1 teaspoon dried Italian herbs
- 2 teaspoons salt
- 1 teaspoon ground black pepper
- ½ teaspoon cayenne pepper
- 1 cup plain bread crumbs
- 1 teaspoon olive oil

**Glaze Ingredients:**

- 2 tablespoons brown sugar
- 2 tablespoons ketchup
- 2 tablespoons dijon mustard
- Hot pepper sauce to taste

**Instructions**

- Preheat the oven to 325 degrees F.
- Place the carrot, celery, onion, red bell pepper, mushrooms, and garlic in a food processor, and pulse until very finely chopped, almost to a puree. Place the minced vegetables into a large mixing bowl, and mix in ground chuck, Worcestershire sauce, and egg. Add Italian herbs, salt, black pepper, and cayenne pepper. Mix gently with a wooden spoon to incorporate vegetables and egg into the meat. Pour in bread crumbs. With your hand, gently mix in the crumbs with your fingertips just until combined, about 1 minute.
- Form the meatloaf into a ball. Pour olive oil into a baking dish and place the ball of meat into the dish. Shape the ball into a loaf, about 4 inches high by 6 inches across.
- Bake in the preheated oven just until the meatloaf is hot, about 15 minutes.
- Meanwhile, in a small bowl, mix together brown sugar, ketchup,

Dijon mustard, and hot sauce. Stir until the brown sugar has dissolved.

- Remove the meatloaf from the oven. With the back of a spoon, smooth the glaze onto the top of the meatloaf, then pull a little bit of glaze down the sides of the meatloaf with the back of the spoon.
- Return meatloaf to the oven, and bake until the loaf is no longer pink inside and the glaze has baked onto the loaf, 30 to 40 more minutes. An instant-read thermometer inserted into the thickest part of the loaf should read at least 160 degrees F (70 degrees C). Cooking time will depend on the shape and thickness of the meatloaf.

**Nutrition Facts**

- Calories: 284; Protein 21.6g; Carbohydrates 14.8g; Fat 14.9g; Cholesterol 85.3mg; Sodium 755.4mg.

# 26. Salisbury Steak

Prep Time: 20 mins Cook Time: 20 mins  Total Time: 40 mins

Servings: 6

### Ingredient

- 1 (10.5 ounces) can condense French onion soup
- 1 ½ pounds ground beef
- ½ cup dry bread crumbs
- 1 egg
- ¼ teaspoon salt
- ⅛ teaspoon ground black pepper
- 1 tablespoon all-purpose flour
- ¼ cup ketchup
- ¼ cup water
- 1 tablespoon Worcestershire sauce
- ½ teaspoon mustard powder

### Instructions

- In a large bowl, mix together 1/3 cup condensed French onion soup with ground beef, bread crumbs, egg, salt, and black pepper. Shape into 6 oval patties.
- In a large skillet over medium-high heat, brown both sides of patties. Pour off excess fat.
- In a small bowl, blend flour and remaining soup until smooth. Mix in ketchup, water, Worcestershire sauce, and mustard powder. Pour over meat in skillet. Cover, and cook for 20 minutes, stirring occasionally.

### Nutrition Facts

- Calories: 440; Protein 23g; Carbohydrates 14.1g; Fat 32.3g; Cholesterol 127.5mg; Sodium 818.3mg.

# 27. **Leek And Pork Stir Fry**

Total Time: 40 mins

## Ingredients

- 1 pound pork shoulder thinly sliced (about 500g)
- 2 Tablespoon oyster sauce
- 2 Tablespoon soy sauce
- 1 Tablespoon sesame oil
- 1 teaspoon garlic powder
- 1 teaspoon onion powder
- 1 teaspoon corn starch
- 1/2 teaspoon black pepper
- 1 cup of leek cleaned and sliced diagonally about 1/2 inch wide

## Instructions

- In a large bowl, mix the pork slices with all the seasoning ingredients. Marinate for at least 30 minutes.
- Lightly grease the inside of the cake barrel.
- Put the marinated pork sliced inside the cake barrel. Air fry at 380F (190C) for about 8 minutes, stirring once in the middle
- Add the leek to the pork and mix. Air fry again at 380F (190C) for another 4-5 minutes until the pork is cooked through.

## Nutrition

- Calories: 186kcal | Carbohydrates: 11g | Protein: 16g | Fat: 9g | Saturated Fat: 2g | Cholesterol: 46mg | Sodium: 814mg | Potassium: 370mg | Fiber: 1g | Sugar: 3g | Vitamin C: 8mg | Calcium: 47mg | Iron: 2mg

# 28.   **Hearty Meatball Soup**

Prep Time: 10 mins

Cook Time: 45 mins

**Ingredients**

**Meatball Ingredients:**

- 1 pound ground meat I used ground turkey, about 500g
- 1/4 cup yellow onion finely chopped
- 1/2 cup Panko breadcrumb
- 1/2 tablespoon Italian seasoning
- 2 tablespoon grated Parmesan cheese
- 1 tablespoon soy sauce
- 2 teaspoon corn starch
- 1 teaspoon garlic powder
- 1 teaspoon onion powder
- 1/4 teaspoon black pepper or to taste

**Soup Ingredients:**

- 2 tablespoon olive oil
- 1 stalk celery diced
- 2 tablespoon garlic chopped
- 1/4 cup yellow onion diced
- 1/4 cup tomato ketchup
- 1/2 cup carrot diced
- 1 large zucchini diced
- 1/4 cup wine I used rice wine
- 1 can crushed tomatoes
- 1/2 can corn kernels
- 2 cup broth I used chicken
- 1 tablespoon Italian seasoning
- 2 teaspoon garlic powder
- Salt and pepper to taste

## Instructions

- Line the fryer basket with a grill mat or a sheet of lightly greased aluminum foil.
- In a large bowl, combine all the meatball ingredients. Take about 1 tablespoonful of the mixture and roll it into a ball. Place the meatballs into the fryer basket. Spritz the meatballs with oil and air fry at 380F (190C) for about 8 minutes, shake the basket once in the middle.
- In the meantime, pour olive oil into a pot and saute garlic, celery, and onion until fragrant. Add in the rest of the soup ingredient and bring it to boil.
- When the meatballs are done, transfer them to the pot. Fill the pot with water just enough to cover all the ingredients. Let it simmer for about 30 minutes.
- Serve on its own or with pasta or bread.

## Nutrition

- Calories: 476kcal | Carbohydrates: 22g | Protein: 24g | Fat: 31g | Saturated Fat: 10g | Cholesterol: 83mg | Sodium: 1047mg | Potassium: 659mg | Fiber: 3g | Sugar: 8g | Vitamin C: 13mg | Calcium: 112mg | Iron: 4mg

# 29.  Easy Swedish Meatballs

Prep Time: 15 mins

Cook Time: 25 mins

## Ingredients

- Ingredients for meatballs: (makes about 30 meatballs)
- 1 1/2 pound ground meat or ground meat mixtures (about 750g) I used ground turkey
- 1/3 cup Panko breadcrumbs
- 1/2 cup milk
- 1/2 of an onion finely chopped
- 1 large egg
- 2 tablespoon parsley dried or fresh
- 2 tablespoon minced garlic
- 1/3 teaspoon salt
- 1/4 teaspoon black pepper or to taste
- 1/4 teaspoon paprika

- 1/4 teaspoon onion powder

**Ingredients For Sauce:**

- 1/3 cup butter
- 1/4 cup all-purpose flour
- 2 cups broth I used chicken broth
- 1/2 cup milk
- 1 tablespoon soy sauce
- Salt and pepper to taste

**Instructions**

- Line the fryer basket with a grill mat or a sheet of lightly greased aluminum foil.
- In a large bowl, combine all the meatball ingredients and let it rest for 5-10 minutes.
- Using the palm of your hands, roll the meat mixture into balls of the desired size. Place them in the fryer basket and air fry at 380F (190C) for 8-12 minutes (depending on the size of the meatballs) until they are cooked through and internal temperature exceeds 165F or 74C)
- In the meantime, melt the butter in a wok or a pan. Whisk in flour until it turns brown. Pour in the broth, milk, and soy sauce and bring it to a simmer. Season with salt and pepper to taste. Stir constantly until the sauce thickens.
- Serve meatballs and sauce over pasta or mashed potato. Sprinkle some parsley if desired.

**Nutrition**

- Calories: 299kcal | Carbohydrates: 12g | Protein: 31g | Fat: 15g | Saturated Fat: 8g | Cholesterol: 121mg | Sodium: 723mg | Potassium: 443mg | Fiber: 1g | Sugar: 3g | Vitamin C: 3mg | Calcium: 71mg | Iron: 2mg

# 30. Garlicky Honey Sesame Ribs

Prep Time: 3 hrs

Cook Time: 15 mins

## Ingredients

- 2 pounds pork ribs about 1000g
- 1/3 cup honey
- 1/4 cup soy sauce
- 1/4 cup ketchup
- 1/4 cup brown sugar
- 2 tbsp rice vinegar
- 2 tbsp lemon juice
- 2 tsp sesame oil
- 2 Tbsp minced garlic
- 1 Tbsp sesame seeds for garnish or to taste
- 1/4 cup scallions for garnish or to taste

## Instructions

- In a medium-size bowl, prepare the marinade by mixing honey, soy sauce, ketchup, brown sugar, vinegar, and lemon juice.
- Take a Ziploc bag, put the ribs in the bag. Pour about 2/3 of the marinade into the bag, mix with the ribs, and marinate in the refrigerator for at least 3 hours or best overnight. Save the rest of the marinade for later use.
- Take the pork ribs out from the refrigerator 30 minutes before air frying.
- Line the fryer basket with a grill mat or a sheet of lightly greased aluminum foil.
- Put the ribs inside the fryer basket without stacking. Air fry at 380F (190C) for about 10-12 minutes, flip once in the middle until the edges are slightly caramelized.
- In the meantime, use a wok to saute garlic in sesame oil until fragrant, about one minute. Then, add in the rest of the marinade. Stir constantly until the sauce thickens.

- When the ribs are done, toss the ribs in the wok along with sesame seeds. Sprinkle some scallions on top to serve.

**Nutrition**

- Calories: 429kcal | Carbohydrates: 30g | Protein: 18g | Fat: 27g | Saturated Fat: 8g | Cholesterol: 85mg | Sodium: 721mg | Potassium: 359mg | Fiber: 1g | Sugar: 27g | Vitamin C: 4mg | Calcium: 46mg | Iron: 2mg

# 31. <u>Chinese BBQ Pork Pastry</u>

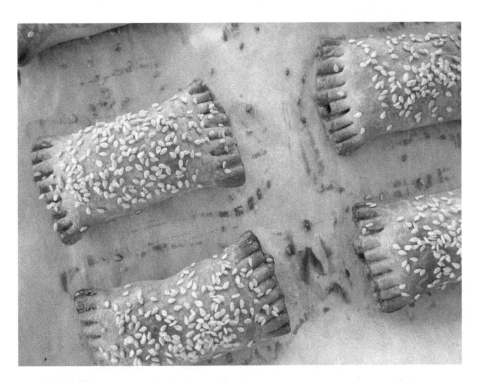

Prep Time: 20 mins

Cook Time: 10 mins

**Ingredients**

- 1/2 pound char siu Chinese BBQ pork diced (about 250g)
- 2 tsp olive oil
- 1/4 onion diced
- 1 1/2 tbsp ketchup
- 1/2 tbsp oyster sauce
- 1 tbsp sugar
- 1 tbsp honey
- 1/4 cup water
- 1 1/2 tbsp corn starch
- 1 1/2 tbsp water

- 1 roll of store-bought pie crust thawed according to package instruction
- 1 egg beaten

## Instructions

- In a wok or frying pan, saute diced onion in olive oil until translucent. Then, add in ketchup, oyster sauce, sugar, honey, and 1/4 cup water. Stir and bring to boil
- In the meantime, take a small bowl and mix the corn starch with 1 1/2 tablespoon of water. Add the mixture to the wok and stir constantly until the sauce thickens.
- Add the diced BBQ pork and stir. Wait for it to cool, then put it in the refrigerator for at least 30 minutes. The refrigeration will cause the mixture to harden and will make it easier to handle later.
- Line the fryer basket with a grill mat or lightly greased aluminum foil.
- Roll out pie crusts. Use a bowl size of your choice to trace circles onto the pie crust and cut them into circular pieces. Mix the leftover pie crust, use a rolling pin to roll them out. Repeat the above process to get as many circular crusts as you can.
- Lay the circular pieces of pie crust on the counter and put the desired amount of BBQ pork filling in the center. Fold pie crust in half and keep the fillings inside. Use the back of a fork to press down on the edges of the pie crust to seal.
- Carefully transfer the pork pastry into the fryer basket. Brush the top surface with egg and air fry at 340F (170C) for about 5-6 minutes. Flip the pastries over and brush the top side with egg. Air fry again at 340F (170C) for another 5-6 minutes until the surface is golden brown.

## Nutrition

- Calories: 225kcal | Carbohydrates: 17g | Protein: 2g | Fat: 7g | Saturated Fat: 2g | Polyunsaturated Fat: 1g | Monounsaturated Fat: 1g | Trans Fat: 1g | Cholesterol: 100mg | Sodium: 395mg | Potassium: 345mg | Fiber: 1g | Sugar: 17g | Vitamin C: 1mg | Calcium: 8mg | Iron: 1mg

# 32. Vietnamese Style Pork Chops

Prep Time: 2 hrs

Cook Time: 10 mins

## Ingredients

- 1 pound pork shoulder blade steak (about 500g)
- 3 tbsp dark soy sauce
- 3 tbsp fish sauce
- 2 tbsp minced garlic
- 2 tbsp grated ginger
- 2 tbsp brown sugar
- 1 Lime juice and zest
- 1 tbsp olive oil
- Chopped cilantro to garnish optional

## Instructions

- Mix the pork with all the pork ingredients, except olive oil and cilantro, and marinate in the refrigerator for at least 2 hours or best overnight. Take the meat out of the refrigerator 30 minutes before air frying.
- Pat dry the pork steaks with a paper towel. Brush both sides of the meat with olive oil and place them in the fryer basket without stacking. Air fry at 400F (200C) for 8-10 minutes, flip once in the middle until the pork is cooked through when the temperature exceeds 145F or 63C.
- Garnish with chopped cilantro if desired.

## Nutrition

- Calories: 229kcal | Carbohydrates: 23g | Protein: 15g | Fat: 9g | Saturated Fat: 2g | Cholesterol: 46mg | Sodium: 1359mg | Potassium: 322mg | Fiber: 1g | Sugar: 17g | Vitamin C: 7mg | Calcium: 33mg | Iron: 1mg

# 33.  **Meatballs With Gochujang Mayo**

Prep Time: 15 mins

Cook Time: 10 mins

**Ingredients**

**Ingredients For Meatballs:**

- 1 pound ground pork (about 500g) or meat of your choice
- 1/4 cup onion finely chopped
- 2 Tablespoon soy sauce

- 2 teaspoon corn starch
- 1 teaspoon dried basil
- 1 teaspoon garlic powder
- 1 teaspoon onion powder
- 1/4 teaspoon white pepper powder

**Ingredients For Sauce:**

- 1 teaspoon Gochujang (Korean hot pepper paste)
- 2 Tablespoon Mayonnaise
- 2 Tablespoon mirin

**Instructions**

- Line the fryer basket with a grill mat or a sheet of lightly greased aluminum foil.
- Mix all the meatball ingredients then form them into about 1 inch balls. Put the meatballs in the fryer basket without stacking. Spray some oil onto the meatballs and air fry at 380F (190C) for 8-10 minutes until the meat is cooked through at its proper temperature.
- In the meantime, take a small bowl and mix all the sauce ingredients.
- Dip the meatballs in the Gochujang mayo to serve.

**Nutrition**

- Calories: 378kcal | Carbohydrates: 7g | Protein: 21g | Fat: 29g | Saturated Fat: 10g | Cholesterol: 85mg | Sodium: 677mg | Potassium: 368mg | Fiber: 1g | Sugar: 3g | Vitamin C: 2mg | Calcium: 21mg | Iron: 1mg

# 34.   <u>Five Spices Salt And Pepper Pork</u>

Prep Time: 1 hr 15 mins

Cook Time: 15 mins

## Ingredients

**Ingredients For Pork:**

- 1/2 pound pork shoulder cut into thick slices (about 250g)
- 2 Tablespoon soy sauce
- 1/2 Tablespoon rice wine
- 1 teaspoon corn starch
- 1 Tablespoon minced garlic
- 1 teaspoon sesame oil
- 1/2 teaspoon sugar
- 1/2 teaspoon Chinese five spices powder
- 1/4 cup tapioca starch

## Instructions

- Marinate the meat with all the pork ingredients, except tapioca flour, for at least 1 hour.
- Dredge the pork slices in tapioca flour, shake off excess, and let sit for about 5-10 minutes until you don't see dry flour.
- Place the meat in the fryer basket and spray some oil. Air Fry at 380F for 12-14 minutes, flip once in the middle until the surface appears to be nice and crisp.
- Toss in the pork slices with chili pepper and chopped cilantro. Then, sprinkle some salt and pepper to serve.

## Nutrition

- Calories: 100kcal | Carbohydrates: 9g | Protein: 8g | Fat: 3g | Saturated Fat: 1g | Cholesterol: 23mg | Sodium: 529mg | Potassium: 137mg | Fiber: 1g | Sugar: 1g | Vitamin C: 1mg | Calcium: 8mg | Iron: 1mg

# 35.  <u>Seasoned Pork Chops With Avocado Salsa</u>

Prep Time: 5 mins

Cook Time: 15 mins

**Ingredients**

- 2 pork chops or pork shoulder blade steaks
- 2 Tablespoon olive oil
- 1 teaspoon sea salt
- 1 teaspoon black pepper

- 1/2 teaspoon paprika
- 1/2 teaspoon garlic powder
- 1/2 teaspoon cumin

## Ingredients For Salsa:

- 1 avocado pitted and diced
- 1 large tomato seeded and diced
- 1/3 cup cilantro chopped
- 1 lime juiced
- 1/4 yellow onion finely chopped
- Pickled or fresh jalapeno to taste chopped (optional)
- Salt to taste

## Instructions

- In a small bowl, mix all the dry seasonings in the pork ingredients and set them aside.
- Use a paper towel to pat dry the pork chop then rub both sides with olive oil. Generously season both sides of the meat and air fry at 380F (190C) for 10-12 minutes, flip once in the middle until the internal temperature exceeds 145F (63C).
- In the meantime, combine all the ingredients for the salsa in a large bowl.
- When the pork chops are done, let them rest for a few minutes. Scoop some salsa over the pork chops to serve.

## Nutrition

- Calories: 528kcal | Carbohydrates: 18g | Protein: 32g | Fat: 38g | Saturated Fat: 7g | Cholesterol: 90mg | Sodium: 1242mg | Potassium: 1187mg | Fiber: 9g | Sugar: 4g | Vitamin C: 30mg | Calcium: 39mg | Iron: 2mg

# 36. **Chinese Style Ground Meat Patties**

Prep Time: 5 mins

Cook Time: 10 mins

## Ingredients

- 1 pound ground pork about 500g
- 1 egg
- 1 teaspoon corn starch
- 1/3 cup green onion chopped
- 1/4 cup cilantro stems chopped
- 1/4 cup yellow onion finely diced
- 2 1/2 Tablespoon oyster sauce
- 2 Tablespoon minced garlic
- 1/4 teaspoon black pepper

## Instructions

- Mix all the ingredients and making sure everything is well combined.
- Line the fryer basket with lightly greased aluminum foil. Form patties of equal size and place them into the fryer basket. Air fry at 380F (190C) for 8-10 minutes until fully cooked when the internal temperature exceeds 160F (72C).

## Nutrition

- Calories: 335kcal | Carbohydrates: 5g | Protein: 21g | Fat: 25g | Saturated Fat: 9g | Cholesterol: 123mg | Sodium: 390mg | Potassium: 394mg | Fiber: 1g | Sugar: 1g | Vitamin C: 5mg | Calcium: 39mg | Iron: 1mg

# 37.  **Pork Satay Skewers**

Prep Time: 1 hr Cook Time: 15 mins

**Ingredients**

**Ingredients For Pork:**

- 1 pound pork shoulder (about 500g) cut into 1/2 inch cubes
- 1/4 cup soy sauce
- 2 Tablespoons brown sugar
- 2 tablespoons Thai sweet chili sauce
- 1 Tablespoon sesame oil
- 1 Tablespoon minced garlic
- 1 Tablespoon fish sauce

**Ingredients For The Sauce:**

- 1/3 cup peanut butter

- 3 Tablespoon coconut milk or milk or water
- 2 Tablespoon Thai Sweet Chili Sauce
- 2 teaspoon minced garlic
- 2 teaspoon brown sugar
- 1 teaspoon fish sauce

## Instructions

- Combine all the ingredients for the pork and marinate for at least 1 hour or overnight.
- In the meantime, soak the wooden skewers in water for at least 15 minutes. Also, combine all the ingredients for the dipping sauce and set aside.
- Thread the pork cubes onto skewers and place them in the fryer basket. Air fry at 380F (190C) for about 8-10 minutes, flip once in between until the meat is cooked through.

## Nutrition

- Calories: 363kcal | Carbohydrates: 23g | Protein: 21g | Fat: 22g | Saturated Fat: 7g | Cholesterol: 46mg | Sodium: 1607mg | Potassium: 444mg | Fiber: 1g | Sugar: 18g | Vitamin C: 2mg | Calcium: 33mg | Iron: 2mg

# 38. Pork Chop Marinated With Fermented Bean Curd

Prep Time: 2 hrs

Cook Time: 15 mins

**Ingredients**

**Ingredients For Pork:**

- 1 pound pork shoulder cut into chunks.
- 1-2 pieces fermented bean curd chunk
- 2 teaspoon rice wine
- 1 Tablespoon dark soy sauce
- 1 Tablespoon brown sugar
- 2 Tablespoon garlic minced
- Other ingredients:
- Fried garlic chips to taste
- Thinly sliced green onions to taste

**Instructions**

- Marinate the pork with all the pork ingredients for at least 2 hours or best overnight in the refrigerator.
- Leave the pork out at room temperature 30 minutes before air frying.
- Line the fryer basket with a sheet of lightly greased aluminum foil. Put the pork inside without stacking and air fry at 380F (190C) for about 10-12 minutes until the temperature exceeds 160F (71C).
- Sprinkle some fried garlic and green onion to serve.

**Nutrition**

- Calories: 143kcal | Carbohydrates: 9g | Protein: 14g | Fat: 5g | Saturated Fat: 2g | Cholesterol: 46mg | Sodium: 194mg | Potassium: 267mg | Fiber: 1g | Sugar: 6g | Vitamin C: 3mg | Calcium: 20mg | Iron: 1mg

# 39. <u>Pork And Bean Curd Strips</u>

Prep Time: 1 hr

Cook Time: 15 mins

**Ingredients**

**Ingredients For Pork:**

- 1/2 pound pork shoulder cut into strips (about 250g)
- 2 teaspoon sesame oil
- 2 teaspoon corn starch
- 1 teaspoon sugar
- 1 Tablespoon rice wine
- Other ingredients:
- 8 ounces bean curd cut into strips
- 1 teaspoon olive oil
- 4-5 cloves of garlic

- 1/4 cup chicken broth
- 3-4 green onion cut into thin slices
- 1 teaspoon black vinegar optional

## Instructions

- Marinate the pork strips with all the pork ingredients for at least one hour or overnight.
- In the meantime, mix 1 teaspoon of olive oil with bean curd strips. In a lightly greased cake pan, air fry the bean curd at 380F (190C) for 6 minutes, stir once in between. Remove and set aside when done.
- Put the garlic on the bottom of the cake pan put pork strips over it. Air fry at 380F (190C) for about 8 minutes, stir once in between.
- Add in the chicken broth, bean curd strips, and half of the green onion and mix. Air fry at 380F (190C) for 4-5 minutes until the pork is cooked through.
- Mix in the remaining green onion and black vinegar to serve.

## Nutrition

- Calories: 143kcal | Carbohydrates: 4g | Protein: 12g | Fat: 8g | Saturated Fat: 2g | Cholesterol: 23mg | Sodium: 83mg | Potassium: 142mg | Fiber: 1g | Sugar: 1g | Vitamin C: 2mg | Calcium: 81mg | Iron:                                                                              1mg

# 40.  Marinated Korean Style Pork With Mushroom

Prep Time: 35 mins

Cook Time: 15 mins

**Ingredients**

**Ingredients For The Pork:**

- 1/2 pound pork shoulder (about 250g) cut into thin slices
- 1/4 cup Korean BBQ sauce

**Other Ingredients:**

- 1 Tablespoon garlic minced
- 1/2 cup button mushroom cut into slices
- 1/3 cup carrots sliced
- 1 Tablespoon Korean BBQ sauce
- 1 teaspoon corn starch
- 1/3 cup green onion cut into 1-inch pieces

**Instructions**

- Marinate the pork with Korean BBQ sauce and set aside for 30 minutes.
- In a lightly greased cake barrel, put the garlic and carrots on the bottom then put pork slices on top. Air fry at 380F (190C) for about 8-9 minutes, stir once in between.
- Mix the rest of the ingredients into the cake pan and air fry again 380F (190C) for 3-4 minutes until pork is cooked through.

**Nutrition**

- Calories: 193kcal | Carbohydrates: 19g | Protein: 17g | Fat: 5g | Saturated Fat: 2g | Cholesterol: 46mg | Sodium: 770mg | Potassium: 426mg | Fiber: 1g | Sugar: 12g | Vitamin C: 7mg | Calcium: 36mg | Iron: 1mg

# 41. **Cilantro Lime Spiced Pork**

Prep Time: 1 hr 10 mins

Cook Time: 15 mins

**Ingredient:**

- 12 Ounces pork shoulder thinly sliced
- 1 Tablespoon soy sauce
- 1/4 teaspoon cumin
- 1/2 teaspoon curry

- 1/4 teaspoon salt

**Other Ingredients:**

- 1/4 cup cilantro chopped
- 3-4 Tablespoon of lime juice or to taste

**Instructions**

- Marinate the pork slices with all the ingredients for at least 1 hour.
- Line the fryer basket with lightly greased aluminum foil. Place the pork slices in the basket and air fry at 380F (190C) for 10-12 minutes until the pork is cooked through.
- When done, mix in cilantro and lime juice to serve.

**Nutrition**

- Calories:162kcal | Carbohydrates: 1g | Protein: 21g | Fat: 8g | Saturated Fat: 3g | Cholesterol: 70mg | Sodium: 874mg | Potassium: 373mg | Sugar: 1g | Vitamin C: 1mg | Calcium: 15mg | Iron: 2mg

# 42. <u>Chinese Style Meatloaf With Pickled Cucumber</u>

Prep Time: 5 mins

Cook Time: 20 mins

**Ingredients For Pork:**

- 1 pound ground pork about 500g
- 1 egg
- 1/4 cup pickled cucumber chopped
- 1 Tablespoon minced garlic
- 1 Tablespoon soy sauce
- 3 Tablespoon juice from pickled cucumber
- 2 teaspoon of rice wine
- 1 teaspoon sesame oil
- 1 teaspoon sugar

- 2 teaspoon corn starch
- White pepper powder to taste

**Other Ingredients:**

- Chicken or beef stock
- 1/4 cup thinly sliced scallions to garnish.

**Instructions**

- Mix all the pork ingredients and scoop the meatloaf into each ramekin and put them inside the fryer basket.
- Fill the stock up to almost to the rim of the ramekins as the fluid may dry up during the air frying process. Put a sheet of aluminum foil over the ramekins and place a steamer rack on top. Air fry at 360F (170C) for about 15-18 minutes until the meat temperature exceeds 160F (72C).
- Sprinkle some green onion on top to serve.

**Nutrition**

- Calories: 336kcal | Carbohydrates: 3g | Protein: 21g | Fat: 26g | Saturated Fat: 9g | Cholesterol: 123mg | Sodium: 331mg | Potassium: 350mg | Sugar: 1g | Vitamin C: 1mg | Calcium: 26mg | Iron: 1mg

# 43.  <u>**Honey Garlic Pork**</u>

Prep Time: 35 mins

Cook Time: 15 mins

**Ingredients For Pork:**

- 1/2 pound pork shoulder thinly sliced
- 1 Tablespoon soy sauce
- 1 teaspoon garlic powder
- 1 teaspoon corn starch
- 1 teaspoon rice wine

- 3 Tablespoon tapioca starch

**Ingredients For Sauce:**

- 1 Tablespoon sesame oil
- 3 Tablespoon minced garlic
- 2 Tablespoon honey
- 2 Tablespoon Chinese black vinegar
- 1 Tablespoon soy sauce

**Instructions**

- In a Ziploc bag, combine all the ingredients for the pork, except for tapioca starch, and marinate for 30 minutes. Before air frying, add tapioca starch to the bag and shake well. The goal is to have all the pork slices coat with some tapioca starch.
- Place a sheet of lightly greased aluminum foil in the fryer basket. Put the pork slices in and try to separate them as much as possible. Air fry at 400F (200C) for about 15 minutes, stir 2-3 times in between until the edges are crispy.
- In the meantime, saute garlic with sesame oil in a saucepan for about one minute. Then combine the rest of the ingredients and stir constantly until the sauce thickens.
- When the pork is done, toss the pork slices in the sauce to serve.

**Nutrition**

- Calories: 154kcal | Carbohydrates: 17g | Protein: 8g | Fat: 6g | Saturated Fat: 1g | Cholesterol: 23mg | Sodium: 531mg | Potassium: 170mg | Fiber: 1g | Sugar: 9g | Vitamin C: 2mg | Calcium: 16mg | Iron: 1mg

# 44. <u>General Tso's Pork</u>

Prep Time: 15 mins

Cook Time: 20 mins

**Ingredients For Pork:**

- 1 pound pork shoulder cut into slices
- 1 egg beaten
- 2 Tablespoon soy sauce
- 1/4 teaspoon salt

- 1/4 teaspoon black pepper
- 1 teaspoon corn starch
- 1/4 cup tapioca starch
- Ingredients for sauce:
- 1 1/2 Tablespoon chili oil
- 2-3 Tablespoon minced garlic
- 1 Tablespoon grated ginger
- 2 Tablespoon soy sauce
- 2 Tablespoon vinegar
- 2 Tablespoon sugar
- 2 teaspoon corn starch mix with 4 teaspoon water

**Instructions**

- In a Ziploc bag, mix all the ingredients for the pork, except tapioca starch, and marinate in the refrigerator for at least one hour. Add the tapioca starch into the bag. Shake the bag or mix gently.
- Line the fryer basket with lightly greased aluminum foil. Put the pork slices in and spread them out as much as possible. Air fry at 400F (200C) for 15-17 minutes until the outside is crispy and the meat is cooked through, stir 2-3 times in between.
- In the meantime, use a saucepan to saute the garlic and ginger in chili oil for one minute. Add in the rest of the ingredients and bring them to a boil. Add in the corn starch and water mixture, stir until the sauce thickens.
- When the pork is done, toss in the sauce to coat. Sprinkle some chopped green onion to serve.

**Nutrition**

- Calories: 235kcal | Carbohydrates: 16g | Protein: 17g | Fat: 11g | Saturated Fat: 3g | Cholesterol: 87mg | Sodium: 1220mg | Potassium: 305mg | Fiber: 1g | Sugar: 6g | Vitamin A: 59IU | Vitamin C: 2mg | Calcium: 23mg | Iron: 2mg

# 45. Korean Marinated Pork Belly

Prep Time: 35 mins

Cook Time: 15 mins

## Ingredients

- 1 pound pork belly with or without skin, (about 500g) cut into thin slices
- 2 Tablespoon minced garlic
- 2 Tablespoon minced ginger
- 1/2 tablespoon Korean hot pepper paste Gochujang, or to taste
- 3 tablespoon honey
- 3 tablespoon soy sauce
- 1 tablespoon sesame oil
- 1/2 tablespoon apple cider vinegar
- 3 tablespoon toasted white sesame seeds

## Instructions

- Prepare the marinade by mixing all other ingredients. Use 3/4 of the marinade to marinate the pork belly for at least 30 minutes and save the rest for later use.
- On a lightly greased aluminum foil, air fry the pork belly slices at 380F (190C) for about 12 minutes, stir about 2 times in between, until the meat is cooked through.
- In the meantime, use a saucepan to heat the remaining marinade on the stovetop. Stir constantly until the sauce thickens. When the pork is done, toss with the sauce.
- To serve, sprinkle some sesame seeds and garnish with cilantro leaves or chopped green onion.

## Nutrition

- Calories: 360kcal | Carbohydrates: 9g | Protein: 7g | Fat: 33g | Saturated Fat: 11g | Cholesterol: 41mg | Sodium: 397mg | Potassium: 149mg | Fiber: 1g | Sugar: 7g | Vitamin C: 1mg | Calcium: 37mg | Iron: 1mg

# 46. Korean Style Pork Chops

Prep Time: 3 hrs

Cook Time: 15 mins

## Ingredients

- 1 pound pork chops (about 500g)
- 1/2 cup soy sauce
- 1/3 cup brown sugar
- 1/3 cup onion thinly sliced
- 2 Tablespoon grated ginger
- 2 Tablespoon minced garlic
- 2 teaspoon sesame oil
- 1 teaspoon black pepper
- 1-2 teaspoon Sriracha hot sauce optional
- 3 Tablespoon sliced green onions
- 1 Tablespoon toasted sesame seeds

## Instructions

- Marinate the pork chops in all the ingredients (except sesame seeds and green onion) in the refrigerator for at least 3 hours. Take the pork chops out of the refrigerator about 30 minutes before air frying.
- Put the pork chops in the parchment paper-lined fryer basket without stacking. Air fry at 380F (190C) for about 15 minutes until the meat temperature is at least 165F (64C).
- Sprinkle some green onion and sesame seeds to serve.

## Nutrition

- Calories: 309kcal | Carbohydrates: 24g | Protein: 28g | Fat: 11g | Saturated Fat: 3g | Cholesterol: 76mg | Sodium: 1709mg | Potassium: 581mg | Fiber: 1g | Sugar: 19g | Vitamin C: 4mg | Calcium: 62mg | Iron: 2mg

# 47. __Char Siu Pork Chops__

Prep Time: 3 hrs

Cook Time: 15 mins

## Ingredients

- 1 pound pork chop about 500g
- 1/3 cup of store-bought char siu sauce see notes for substitution
- 2 Tablespoon soy sauce

## Instructions

- Marinate the pork chops in all the ingredients. Refrigerate for at least 3 hours. Take the pork chops out of the refrigerator 30 minutes before air frying.
- Place the pork chops in the parchment paper-lined fryer basket and air fry at 380F (190C) for about 15 minutes until the meat temperature is at least 165F (64C).

## Nutrition

- Calories: 206kcal | Carbohydrates: 7g | Protein: 25g | Fat: 8g | Saturated Fat: 3g | Polyunsaturated Fat: 1g | Monounsaturated Fat: 1g | Trans Fat: 1g | Cholesterol: 76mg | Sodium: 1032mg | Potassium: 442mg | Fiber: 1g | Sugar: 1g | Calcium: 8mg | Iron: 1mg

# 48.  <u>Wasabi Lime Steak</u>

Prep Time: 1 hr 15 mins

Cook Time: 15 mins

### Ingredients for the steak:

- 1 pound flank steak (about 500g) thinly sliced
- 1 tablespoon wasabi paste
- 2 Tablespoon soy sauce
- 2 Tablespoon lime juice
- 1/2 Tablespoon Sesame oil
- 1 Tablespoon grated ginger

### Wasabi Mayonnaise:

- 1/4 cup mayonnaise
- 1 Tablespoon water
- 1 Tablespoon mirin non-alcohol
- 1 Tablespoon lime juice

- 1 teaspoon wasabi paste
- Other ingredients:
- 1/3 cup cilantro chopped

## Instructions

- Combine all the ingredients for the steak and mix well. Marinate for at least one hour or overnight in the refrigerator.
- Line the fryer basket with a sheet of lightly greased aluminum foil. Spread the beef slices out as much as possible and air fry at 380F (190C) for about 8-10 minutes, stir 1-2 times in between.
- In the meantime, mix the mayonnaise, water, mirin, lime juice, and wasabi paste in a medium bowl.
- Drizzle the wasabi mayo over the steak and garnish with some cilantro to serve.

## Nutrition

- Calories: 288kcal | Carbohydrates: 5g | Protein: 26g | Fat: 18g | Saturated Fat: 4g | Cholesterol: 74mg | Sodium: 686mg | Potassium: 427mg | Fiber: 1g | Sugar: 2g | Vitamin C: 6mg | Calcium: 29mg | Iron: 2mg

# 49.   Korean Beef With Veggie

Prep Time: 40 mins

Cook Time:15 mins

**Ingredients For Beef:**

12 ounces flank steak cut into thin slices

1 teaspoon corn starch

1/4 cup Korean BBQ sauce

**Other Ingredients:**

- 2 cups mung bean sprouts
- 3 cups baby spinach or spinach cut into 2-inch length
- 1 Tablespoon sesame oil
- 1 Tablespoon minced garlic

- 1 Tablespoon freshly grated ginger
- 1 Tablespoon rice wine
- 2-3 Tablespoon Korean BBQ sauce
- 1 teaspoon jalapeno pepper sliced (optional)
- 1 teaspoon toasted sesame seeds

## Instructions

- In a large bowl, marinate the beef with Korean BBQ sauce and corn starch for about 30 minutes.
- In a small pot, boil the mung bean sprouts until tender. Remove and set aside. Then, boil the spinach for about one minute and set aside.
- In a lightly greased cake pan, air fry the marinated beef at 380F (190C) for about 7-8 minutes, stir once in between.
- In the meantime, stir fry the garlic, grated ginger, and jalapeno pepper with sesame oil in a wok for about 1-2 minutes until fragrant. Add in the Korean BBQ sauce and rice wine and bring to a boil then turn the stove off.
- Toss the spinach, bean sprouts, and beef slices in the sauce. Sprinkle some sesame seeds over the dish to serve.

## Nutrition

- Calories:220kcal | Carbohydrates: 13g | Protein: 22g | Fat: 8g | Saturated Fat: 2g | Cholesterol: 51mg | Sodium: 486mg | Potassium: 493mg | Fiber: 1g | Sugar: 9g | Vitamin C: 15mg | Calcium: 55mg | Iron: 2mg

# 50. <u>Mongolian Beef</u>

Prep Time: 15 mins

Cook Time: 10 mins

**Ingredients For The Beef:**

- 1 pound flank steak cut into 1/4 inch thick pieces (about 500g)
- 2 teaspoon soy sauce
- 1 teaspoon sesame oil
- 2 teaspoon cornstarch
- 1/4 cup tapioca starch

**Ingredients For The Sauce:**

- 2 Tablespoon olive oil
- 1 Tablespoon grated ginger
- 1 Tablespoon minced garlic
- 2 Tablespoon soy sauce
- 3 Tablespoon brown sugar

- 3-4 green onion green parts only, cut into 1-2 inch pieces
- 1-2 teaspoon sesame seeds optional

## Instructions

- In a Ziploc back, marinate the steak pieces with soy sauce, sesame oil, and corn starch for at least 15 minutes. Add in the tapioca starch and shake, making sure all the pieces are coated.
- Line the fryer basket with a sheet of lightly greased aluminum foil. Put the steak pieces in, preferably without stacking, and air fry at 400F (200C) for about 8 minutes, flip once until the edges look slightly crispy.
- In the meantime, in a frying pan or a wok, saute the garlic and grated ginger in olive oil for about 1-2 minutes until fragrant. Add in the soy sauce and brown sugar and stir constantly until the sauce thickens.
- When the beef is done, toss the beef in the sauce, followed by the green onion. To serve, sprinkle the dish with sesame seeds if desired.

## Nutrition

- Calories: 306kcal | Carbohydrates: 19g | Protein: 26g | Fat: 14g | Saturated Fat: 4g | Cholesterol: 68mg | Sodium: 735mg | Potassium: 443mg | Fiber: 1g | Sugar: 9g | Vitamin A: 90IU | Vitamin C: 2mg | Calcium: 46mg | Iron: 2mg

# 51.   <u>Beef Wrapped Cheesy Mushroom</u>

Prep Time: 10 mins

Cook Time: 10 mins

## Ingredients

- 12 pieces of thinly sliced beef
- 12 button mushrooms
- 1/3 cup cheddar cheese
- 1/4 cup Korean BBQ sauce
- 2 Tablespoon sesame seeds optional
- 6 pieces of pickled jalapeno peppers chopped (optional)

## Instructions

- Marinate the beef with Korean BBQ sauce for 15 minutes.
- Use a paper towel to wipe the button mushroom clean and remove the stems. Fill the mushroom with cheese and some chopped jalapeno pepper.
- Take a slice of beef and wrap it around the mushroom. Air fry at 380F (190C) for about 5 minutes (depending on the thickness of the meat).
- Sprinkle some sesame seeds to serve.

## Nutrition

- Calories: 330kcal | Carbohydrates: 16g | Protein: 29g | Fat: 17g | Saturated Fat: 7g | Cholesterol: 73mg | Sodium: 800mg | Potassium: 718mg | Fiber: 2g | Sugar: 11g | Vitamin C: 3mg | Calcium: 214mg | Iron: 4mg

# 52. Cumin Beef

Prep Time: 3 hrs

Cook Time:15 mins

## Ingredients

- 1 pound beef flank steak thinly sliced (about 500g)
- 3 Tablespoon Soy sauce
- 2 Tablespoon chopped garlic
- 1 tablespoon Shaoxing wine

- 1 1/2 Tablespoon cumin
- 1 Tablespoon paprika
- 1 1/2 teaspoon corn starch
- 1/4 teaspoon salt
- 1/2 teaspoon black pepper
- 1/2 teaspoon hot pepper flakes optional
- 1/3 cup chopped cilantro
- 1/2 cup chopped green onion

**Instructions**

- Marinate the beef slices with all of the ingredients, except cilantro and green onion, in the refrigerator for at least 3 hours. Remove from the refrigerator about 30 minutes before air frying.
- In a lightly greased foiled lined fryer basket, air fry the beef slices at 380F (190C), stir 2-3 times in between, about 10-12 minutes, or until the desired degree of doneness is reached.
- When done, toss the beef with cilantro and green onion to serve.

**Nutrition**

- Calories: 196kcal | Carbohydrates: 6g | Protein: 27g | Fat: 6g | Saturated Fat: 2g | Cholesterol: 68mg | Sodium: 968mg | Potassium: 546mg | Fiber: 1g | Sugar: 1g | Vitamin A: 1105IU | Vitamin C: 4mg | Calcium: 68mg | Iron: 4mg

# 53. Meatballs With Gochujang Mayo

Prep Time: 15 mins

Cook Time: 10 mins

## Ingredients For Meatballs:

- 1 pound ground pork (about 500g) or meat of your choice
- 1/4 cup onion finely chopped
- 2 Tablespoon soy sauce
- 2 teaspoon corn starch
- 1 teaspoon dried basil
- 1 teaspoon garlic powder
- 1 teaspoon onion powder
- 1/4 teaspoon white pepper powder
- Ingredients for sauce:
- 1 teaspoon Gochujang (Korean hot pepper paste)
- 2 Tablespoon Mayonnaise
- 2 Tablespoon mirin

## Instructions

- Line the fryer basket with a grill mat or a sheet of lightly greased aluminum foil.
- Mix all the meatball ingredients then form them into about 1 inch balls. Put the meatballs in the fryer basket without stacking. Spray some oil onto the meatballs and air fry at 380F (190C) for 8-10 minutes until the meat is cooked through at its proper temperature.
- In the meantime, take a small bowl and mix all the sauce ingredients.
- Dip the meatballs in the Gochujang mayo to serve.

## Nutrition

- Calories:378kcal | Carbohydrates: 7g | Protein: 21g | Fat: 29g | Saturated Fat: 10g | Cholesterol: 85mg | Sodium: 677mg | Potassium: 368mg | Fiber: 1g | Sugar: 3g | Vitamin C: 2mg | Calcium: 21mg | Iron: 1mg

# 54. <u>Pie Crust Beef Empanadas</u>

Prep Time: 30 mins

Cook Time: 15 mins

**Ingredients**

- 1 pound ground beef
- 1-2 Tablespoon pickled jalapeno chopped (optional)
- 1 teaspoon corn starch
- 1 teaspoon cumin

- 1 teaspoon chili powder
- 1/4 teaspoon salt or to taste
- 1/4 teaspoon pepper or to taste
- 1 teaspoon olive oil
- 2 Tablespoon minced garlic
- 1/4 cup diced onions
- 2 rolls of pie crust thawed according to package instruction
- 1 cup Mexican blend cheese or to taste
- 1 egg beaten

## Instructions

- In a large bowl, mix the ground beef with jalapeno (optional), corn starch, cumin, chili powder, salt, and pepper, and let it sit for about 5-10 minutes.
- Line the fryer basket with a grill mat or lightly greased aluminum foil.
- In a large skillet, saute garlic and onion for about 1 minute until fragrant. Add in the ground beef and stir fry until beef is cooked through and the onion is translucent.
- Roll out pie crusts. Use a bowl size of your choice to trace circles onto the piecrust and cut them into circular pieces. Mix the leftover pie crust, use a rolling pin to roll them out. Repeat the above process to get as many circular crusts as you can.
- Lay the circular pieces of pie crust on the counter and put the desired amount of filling and cheese in the center. Fold pie crust in half and keep the fillings inside. Use the back of a fork to press down on the edges of the pie crust.
- Carefully transfer the empanadas into the fryer basket. Brush the top surface with egg and air fry at 350F (175C) for about 4-5 minutes. Flip the empanadas over and brush the top side with egg. Air fry again at 350F (175C) for another 3-4 minutes until the surface is golden brown.

## Nutrition

- Calories: 545kcal | Carbohydrates: 30g | Protein: 22g | Fat: 37g | Saturated Fat: 14g | Cholesterol: 99mg | Sodium: 554mg | Potassium: 318mg | Fiber: 2g | Sugar: 1g | Vitamin C: 1mg | Calcium: 159mg | Iron: 4mg

# 55. Tri-tip Roast

Prep Time: 1 hr 10 mins

Cook Time: 30 mins

**Ingredients**

- 2 pound tri-tip roast excess fat trimmed
- 6-8 garlic cloves
- 1/4 cup olive oil
- 2 1/2 tsp salt
- 1 tsp garlic powder
- 1/2 tsp black pepper

**Instructions**

- In a food processor or a blender, pulse the seasoning ingredient several times.
- Pat dry the tri-tip roast with a paper towel and put it inside a large Ziploc bag.
- Put the seasoning mixture inside the bag, squeeze out as much air as possible and seal the bag. Spread the seasoning and massage the meat at the same time, making sure all surfaces are covered with the mixture. Leave it at room temperature for about one hour.
- Insert a meat thermometer into the center of the roast. Air fry at 400F (200C) for about 20-25 minutes until the desired temperature is reached, 125F (52C) for rare, 135F (57C) for medium-rare and 145F (63C) for medium.
- Let the roast rest for about 10 minutes before serving.

**Nutrition**

- Calories:323kcal | Carbohydrates: 1g | Protein: 31g | Fat: 21g | Saturated Fat: 6g | Cholesterol: 98mg | Sodium: 1050mg | Potassium: 503mg | Fiber: 1g | Sugar: 1g | Vitamin C: 1mg | Calcium: 42mg | Iron: 2mg

# 56.  <u>**Cheese Stuffed Meatballs**</u>

Prep Time: 10 mins

Cook Time: 15 mins

**Ingredients**

- 1 lb ground beef (about 500g)
- 3/4 cup crushed saltine crackers or breadcrumb
- 1/4 cup onion chopped
- 1/4 cup Parmesan cheese

- 1 tsp onion powder
- 1 tsp garlic powder
- 1 tsp parsley
- 1/2 tsp salt
- 1/4 tsp pepper
- 2 eggs
- 3 sticks mozzarella cheese cut into 4-5 pieces each

**Other Ingredients:**

- Spaghetti sauce

**Instructions**

- Line the fryer basket with a grill mat or lightly greased aluminum foil.
- Mix all the ingredients, except mozzarella cheese. Scoop about 2 Tablespoons of the meat mixture and wrap one piece of the cheese in the middle to form a ball. Place the meatballs inside the air fryer.
- Spray the meatballs with some oil. Air fry at 380F (190C) for about 6 minutes. Flip, spray some oil again, and air fry at 380F (190C) for another 4-5 minutes.
- Take a pot to heat the spaghetti sauce. When the meatballs are done, simmer the meatballs in the sauce for a few minutes.
- Serve the meatballs and sauce with your favorite pasta.

**Nutrition**

- Calories: 312kcal | Carbohydrates: 9g | Protein: 20g | Fat: 21g | Saturated Fat: 9g | Cholesterol: 119mg | Sodium: 532mg | Potassium: 254mg | Fiber: 1g | Sugar: 1g | Vitamin A: 112IU | Vitamin C: 1mg | Calcium: 83mg | Iron: 2mg

# 57. **Asian Meatball Stuffed Zucchini**

Prep Time: 15 mins

Cook Time: 15 mins

## Ingredients

- 1 pound ground beef (about 500g)
- 1 egg beaten
- 1/4 cup minced onion
- 2 tbsp chopped basil
- 2 tbsp oyster sauce
- 1 tsp corn starch
- 1/4 tsp black pepper or to taste
- 2 large zucchinis peeled

## Instructions

- Combine all the ingredients, except zucchini, and let it marinate at room temperature for about 15 minutes.
- Line the fryer basket with a large sheet of aluminum and spray it with some oil.
- Cut zucchini into 1-inch sections and hollow out the center with a sharp knife. Then, fill the zucchini with the beef mixture and put them into the fryer basket without stacking.
- Air fry at 360F (180C) for 10-12 minutes. Flip sides about halfway through and continue to air fry until the ground meat is cooked through when then internal temperature exceeds 160F (72C).

## Nutrition

- Calories: 221kcal | Carbohydrates: 4g | Protein: 15g | Fat: 16g | Saturated Fat: 6g | Cholesterol: 81mg | Sodium: 231mg | Potassium: 394mg | Fiber: 1g | Sugar: 2g | Vitamin C: 12mg | Calcium: 30mg | Iron: 2mg

# 58.  Air Fried Bulgogi

Prep Time: 30 mins

Cook Time: 10 mins

## Ingredients

- 1 pound thinly sliced beef rib-eye
- 1/4 cup thinly sliced onion
- 1/3 cup Korean BBQ Sauce or to taste
- 2 tbsp grated ginger
- 1/4 cup thinly sliced green onion
- 2 tsp sesame seed

## Instructions

- In a large Ziploc bag, combine the meat, onion, Korean BBQ sauce, and ginger and mix well. Marinate for at least 30 minutes.
- Lin the fryer basket with a grill mat or a sheet of lightly greased aluminum foil.
- Spread the beef out inside the basket as much as possible and air fry at 380F (190C) for 8-10 minutes, stir once in the middle until the meat is cooked through.
- Sprinkle with sesame seeds and green onion to serve.

## Nutrition

Calories: 283kcal | Carbohydrates: 9g | Protein: 24g | Fat: 17g | Saturated Fat: 7g | Cholesterol: 69mg | Sodium: 433mg | Potassium: 361mg | Fiber: 1g | Sugar: 6g | Vitamin C: 2mg | Calcium: 22mg | Iron: 2mg

# 59.  **Black Pepper Steak And Mushroom**

Prep Time: 1 hr 15 mins

Cook Time: 15 mins

**Ingredients For Steak:**

- 1 pound rib eye steak about 500g, cubed (about 1/2 inch pieces)
- 1 tsp cornstarch
- 1 tbsp rice wine
- 1 tbsp lime juice
- 2 tsp light soy sauce
- 2 tsp dark soy sauce
- 2 tbsp grated ginger
- 1/4 tsp black pepper or to taste

**Other Ingredients:**

- 8 button mushrooms thinly sliced
- 1 tbsp garlic finely chopped
- 1 tbsp oyster sauce

## Instructions

- In a Ziploc bag, mix all the ingredients for the steak and marinate for about one hour.
- Line the fryer basket with a sheet of lightly greased aluminum foil.
- Put the steak inside the fryer basket and air fry at 380F (190C) for about 5 minutes.
- Add all other ingredients to the steak and stir. Air fry at 380F (190C) for another 4-5 minutes or until the desired doneness is reached.
- Carefully pour the drippings from aluminum foil into a wok and bring it to a boil. Stir constantly until the sauce thickens.
- Toss the steak cubes in the wok to coat. Serve immediately.

## Nutrition

- Calories:275kcal | Carbohydrates: 7g | Protein: 25g | Fat: 16g | Saturated Fat: 7g | Cholesterol: 69mg | Sodium: 407mg | Potassium: 446mg | Fiber: 1g | Sugar: 3g | Vitamin C: 3mg | Calcium: 12mg | Iron: 2mg

# 60.  <u>Marinated Rib-Eye Steak</u>

Prep Time: 2 hrs

Cook Time: 10 mins

**Ingredients**

- 1 pound rib-eye steak (or any cut you prefer) 500g
- 2 Tablespoon grated Ginger
- 2 Tablespoon Honey
- 1 Tablespoon minced garlic
- 1 Tablespoon sesame oil
- 2 teaspoon apple cider vinegar
- 1/4 cup soy sauce
- 1 teaspoon scallion optional
- 1 teaspoon dried minced garlic optional

**Instructions**

- Combine all the seasoning ingredients, except scallions and fried minced garlic, and marinate the steak in a Ziploc bag for at least 2 hours or best overnight in the refrigerator.
- If refrigerated, remove from the fridge about 30 minutes before air frying.
- Preheat air fryer for 400F (200C) for 3-4 minutes.
- Place the steak in the preheated air fryer and air fry at 400F (200C) for 6-8 minutes, flip once in the middle, until the desired doneness is reached.
- Let the steak rest for about 10 minutes before cutting. Sprinkle some fried minced garlic and scallions to serve if desired.

**Nutrition**

- Calories: 317kcal | Carbohydrates: 11g | Protein: 25g | Fat: 20g | Saturated Fat: 8g | Cholesterol: 69mg | Sodium: 870mg | Potassium: 349mg | Fiber: 1g | Sugar: 9g | Vitamin C: 1mg | Calcium: 19mg | Iron: 2mg

# 61.   Asian Flavored Ribs

Prep Time: 2 hrs 15 mins

Cook Time: 10 mins

## Ingredients

- 1 pound beef short ribs about 500g
- 1/3 cup brown sugar
- 1/4 cup oyster sauce
- 1/4 cup soy sauce
- 2 tbsp rice wine
- 3 cloves garlic minced
- 1 tbsp fresh grated ginger
- 1 tbsp scallions

## Instructions

- Put the short ribs in a large Ziploc bag.
- In a large bowl, mix all other ingredients, except scallions. Pour the mixture into the Ziploc bag and mix it with the ribs. Marinate the ribs for about 2 hours.
- Line the fryer basket with a sheet of lightly greased aluminum foil.
- Place the ribs inside the fryer basket, without stacking. Air fry at 380F (190C) for 8-10 minutes, flip once in the middle until the surface is slightly caramelized.
- Sprinkle some scallions to garnish.

## Nutrition

Calories: 244kcal | Carbohydrates: 22g | Protein: 18g | Fat: 9g | Saturated Fat: 4g | Cholesterol: 49mg | Sodium: 867mg | Potassium: 360mg | Fiber: 1g | Sugar: 18g | Vitamin C: 1mg | Calcium: 33mg | Iron: 2mg

# 62.   Korean Ground Beef Stir Fry

Prep Time: 5 mins

Cook Time: 10 mins

## Ingredients

- 1/2 pound ground beef (or ground meat of your choice) about 500g
- 1 teaspoon corn starch
- 1/4 cup Korean BBQ sauce (**see note) or to taste
- 1/4 cup zucchini julienned
- 1/4 cup steamed carrots julienned
- 1 tablespoon sesame seeds
- 1/4 cup scallions

## Instructions

- In a large bowl, mix the ground beef, corn starch, and Korean BBQ sauce. Marinate for about 5 minutes.
- Add the carrots and zucchini to the bowl, and gently mix.
- Transfer the mixture to a lightly greased cake barrel and use a spatula to spread them out a bit. Air fry at 380F (190C) for 8-10 minutes, stirring twice in the middle until the ground beef is cooked through.
- Sprinkle some sesame seeds and scallions to serve.

## Nutrition

- Calories: 189kcal | Carbohydrates: 7g | Protein: 11g | Fat: 12g | Saturated Fat: 5g | Cholesterol: 40mg | Sodium: 325mg | Potassium: 226mg | Fiber: 1g | Sugar: 5g | Vitamin C: 3mg | Calcium: 37mg | Iron: 1mg

# 63. <u>Swedish Meatballs</u>

Prep Time: 15 mins Cook Time: 25 mins

**Ingredients For Meatballs: (Makes About 30 Meatballs)**

- 1 1/2 pound ground meat or ground meat mixtures (about 750g) I used ground turkey
- 1/3 cup Panko breadcrumbs
- 1/2 cup milk
- 1/2 of an onion finely chopped
- 1 large egg

- 2 tablespoon parsley dried or fresh
- 2 tablespoon minced garlic
- 1/3 teaspoon salt
- 1/4 teaspoon black pepper or to taste
- 1/4 teaspoon paprika
- 1/4 teaspoon onion powder

**Ingredients For Sauce:**

- 1/3 cup butter
- 1/4 cup all-purpose flour
- 2 cups broth I used chicken broth
- 1/2 cup milk
- 1 tablespoon soy sauce
- Salt and pepper to taste

**Instructions**

- Line the fryer basket with a grill mat or a sheet of lightly greased aluminum foil.
- In a large bowl, combine all the meatball ingredients and let it rest for 5-10 minutes.
- Using the palm of your hands, roll the meat mixture into balls of the desired size. Place them in the fryer basket and air fry at 380F (190C) for 8-12 minutes (depending on the size of the meatballs) until they are cooked through and internal temperature exceeds 165F or 74C)
- In the meantime, melt the butter in a wok or a pan. Whisk in flour until it turns brown. Pour in the broth, milk, and soy sauce and bring it to a simmer. Season with salt and pepper to taste. Stir constantly until the sauce thickens.
- Serve meatballs and sauce over pasta or mashed potato. Sprinkle some parsley if desired.

**Nutrition**

- Calories: 299kcal | Carbohydrates: 12g | Protein: 31g | Fat: 15g | Saturated Fat: 8g | Cholesterol: 121mg | Sodium: 723mg | Potassium: 443mg | Fiber: 1g | Sugar: 3g | Vitamin C: 3mg | Calcium: 71mg | Iron: 2mg

# 64.   <u>Korean Kimchi Beef</u>

Prep Time: 30 mins

Cook Time: 10 mins

## Ingredients For Beef:

- 1 pound tri-tip strip about 500g, thinly sliced
- 1/4 cup kimchi juice
- 1 tablespoon oyster sauce
- 1 tablespoon soy sauce
- 1 tablespoon freshly grated ginger
- 1 teaspoon sesame oil
- 1 teaspoon corn starch

## Other Ingredients:

- 1/2 cup kimchi or to taste
- 1/4 cup thinly sliced green onion
- 1 teaspoon sesame seeds optional

## Instructions

- In a large bowl, combine all the beef ingredients and marinate for at least 30 minutes.
- Line the fryer basket with a sheet of lightly greased aluminum foil.
- Transfer the content of the bowl to the fryer basket and air fry at 380F (190C) for 5 minutes. Stir once in the middle.
- Add the kimchi and green onion to the beef and stir. Air fry again at 380F (190C) for about 3 minutes.
- Sprinkle some toasted sesame seeds to serve if desired.

## Nutrition

- Calories: 200kcal | Carbohydrates: 2g | Protein: 24g | Fat: 10g | Saturated Fat: 3g | Cholesterol: 74mg | Sodium: 436mg | Potassium: 391mg | Fiber: 1g | Sugar: 1g | Vitamin C: 1mg | Calcium: 37mg | Iron: 2mg

# 65. <u>Beef And Macaroni Hotdish</u>

Prep: 15 mins Cook: 25 mins Total: 40 mins

## Ingredient

- 1 pound ground beef
- 2 cups elbow macaroni
- ½ large green bell pepper, coarsely chopped
- ½ large onion, chopped
- 1 (16 ounces) can tomato sauce
- 1 pound tomatoes, coarsely chopped
- 2 teaspoons Worcestershire sauce
- 1 teaspoon soy sauce
- 1 teaspoon salt
- ¾ teaspoon dried basil
- ¾ teaspoon dried oregano
- ½ teaspoon ground black pepper
- ½ teaspoon chili powder
- ¼ teaspoon garlic powder
- ⅛ teaspoon hot pepper sauce (such as Tabasco®)
- 1 cup beef broth

## Instructions

- Cook beef in a large skillet over medium heat, stirring occasionally, until browned, about 5 minutes. Transfer beef to a bowl.
- Cook macaroni, bell pepper, and onion in the same skillet over medium heat for 3 minutes. Add cooked beef, tomato sauce, tomatoes, Worcestershire sauce, soy sauce, salt, basil, oregano, ground black pepper, chili powder, garlic powder, and hot pepper sauce. Pour in beef broth. Cover skillet and simmer until macaroni is tender about 15 minutes. Remove lid and simmer, stirring occasionally, until thickened, 5 to 10 minutes.

## Nutrition Facts

- Calories:336| Protein:19.6g| Carbohydrates:35.9g| Fat:12.8g| Cholesterol: 46.4mg| Sodium: 1039.5mg.

# 66. __Tennessee Meatloaf__

Prep Time: 40 mins

Cook Time: 1 hr

Additional Time: 15 mins

Total Time: 1 hr 55 mins

**Ingredients**

**Brown Sugar Glaze:**

- ½ cup ketchup
- ¼ cup brown sugar
- 2 tablespoons cider vinegar

## Meatloaf:

- Cooking spray
- 1 onion, chopped
- ½ green bell pepper, chopped
- 2 cloves garlic, minced
- 2 large eggs, lightly beaten
- 1 teaspoon dried thyme
- 1 teaspoon seasoned salt
- ½ teaspoon ground black pepper
- 2 teaspoons prepared mustard
- 2 teaspoons worcestershire sauce
- ½ teaspoon hot pepper sauce (such as tabasco®)
- ½ cup milk
- ⅔ cup quick-cooking oats
- 1 pound ground beef
- ½ pound ground pork
- ½ pound ground veal

## Instructions

- Combine ketchup, brown sugar, and cider vinegar in a bowl; mix well.
- Preheat oven to 350 degrees F (175 degrees C). Spray two 9x5-inch loaf pans with cooking spray or line with aluminum foil for easier cleanup (see Cook's Note).
- Place onion and green pepper in a covered microwave container and cook until softened, 1 to 2 minutes. Set aside to cool.
- In a large mixing bowl, combine garlic, eggs, thyme, seasoned salt, black pepper, mustard, Worcestershire sauce, hot sauce, milk, and oats. Mix well. Stir in cooked onion and green pepper. Add ground beef, pork, and veal. With gloved hands, work all ingredients together until completely mixed and uniform.
- Divide meatloaf mixture in half and pat half of mixture into each prepared loaf pan. Brush loaves with half of the glaze; set the remainder of glaze aside.

- Bake in preheated oven for 50 minutes. Remove pans from oven; carefully drain fat. Brush loaves with remaining glaze. Return to oven and bake for 10 minutes more. Remove pans from the oven and allow the meatloaf to stand for 15 minutes before slicing.

**Nutrition Facts**

- Calories: 233| Protein: 17.1g| Carbohydrates: 15.9g| Fat: 11.2g|Cholesterol: 92mg|

CPSIA information can be obtained
at www.ICGtesting.com
Printed in the USA
BVHW091217040521
606415BV00003B/604